2nd Edition

LET'S GO
to the English World
2

Phonics

Short Vowels

CHUNJAE EDUCATION, INC.

CONTENTS

Appendix   Phonics Words
Readers
Flashcards
Stickers

Workbook

Short Vowel a

● **Listen and repeat.** 01

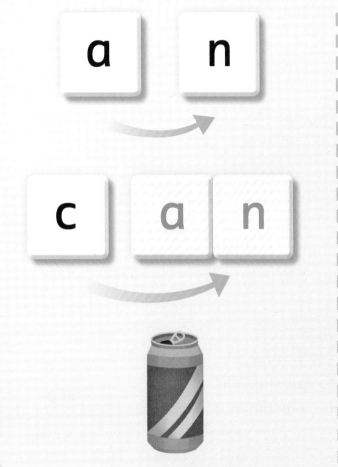

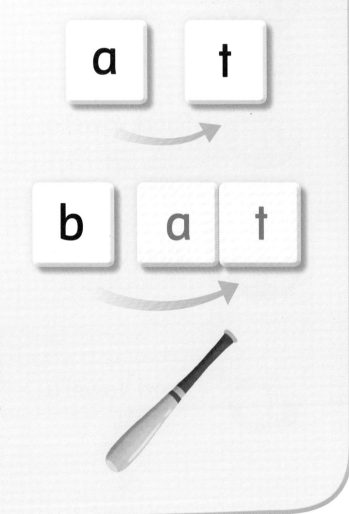

A **Read step by step.**

1.

2.

B Read and say. 02

an

fan

man

pan

at

cat

hat

mat

C Point and chant. 03

an

at

1.  c | an

2.  m | sticker

3.  h | sticker

4.  p | sticker

5. 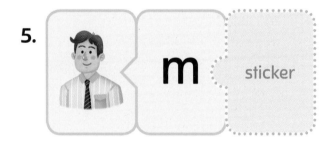 m | sticker

6. 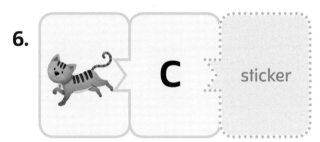 c | sticker

7. 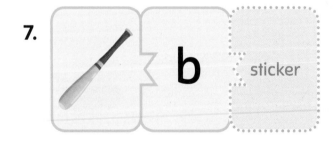 b | sticker

8.  f | sticker

Say aloud. ❶ ❷ ❸

B **Match and write.**

1.

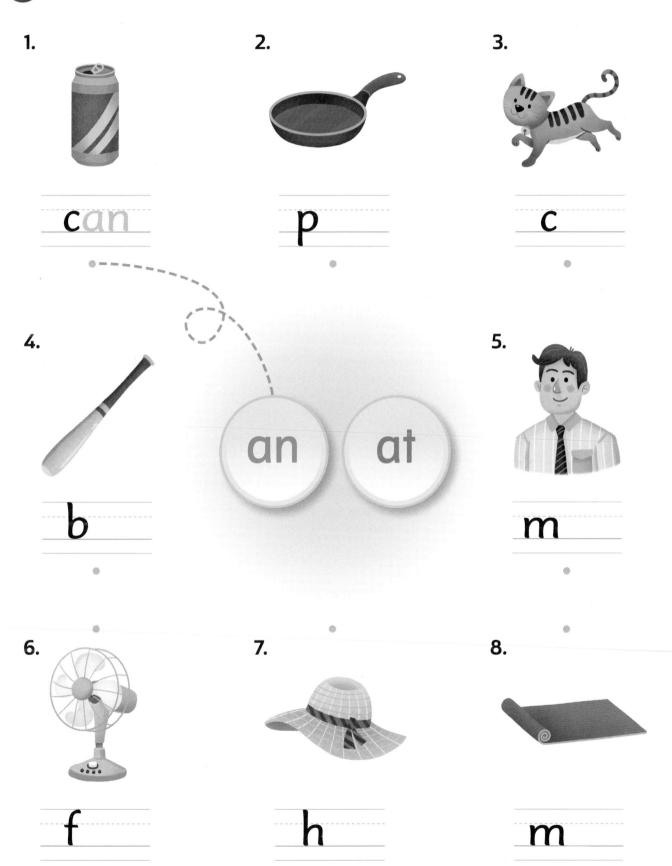

c an

2.

p

3.

c

4.

b

an   at

5.

m

6.

f

7.

h

8.

m

A Listen and check.

1.

2.

3.

B Listen and circle. 06

1.    A (cat / hat) is on the mat.

2.    A (fan / can) is in the pan.

3.    A (bat / hat) is on the man.

C Find and circle.

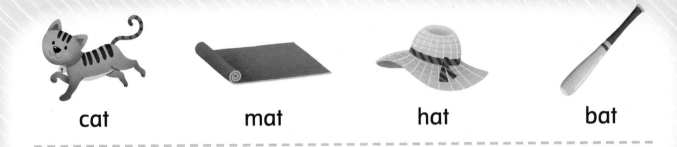

cat   mat   hat   bat

pan   fan   man   can

● **Let's read together.** 07

The hat is on the mat.

The fan is on the mat.

The hat is on the pan.

Oh, it's my hat.

Sight Words

the   is   on   my

Writing Time

● **Write and say.**

1. c + an ➡ can

2. f + an ➡ fan

3. m + an ➡ man

4.  p + an ➡ pan

5. b + at ➡ bat

6. c + at ➡ cat

7.  h + at ➡ hat

8. m + at ➡ mat

➡ Go to the workbook p. 2 **11**

Short Vowel a

● **Listen and repeat.** 08

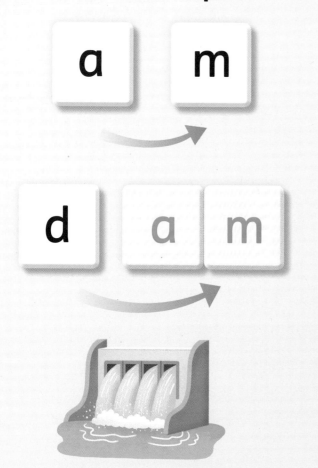

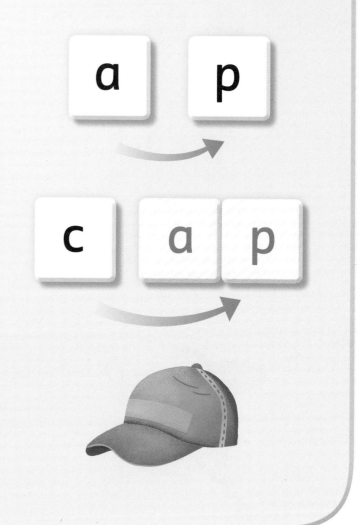

A **Read step by step.**

1.

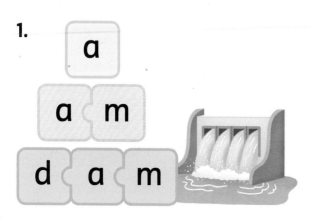

2.

B Read and say. 09

am

ham   jam   ram

ap

map   nap   tap

C Point and chant. 10

am

ap

A Listen and color. 🎧11

1.  t / d **ap**

2.  c / k **ap**

3.  l / r **am**

4. 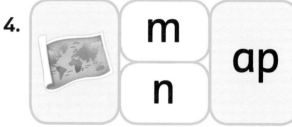 m / n **ap**

5. 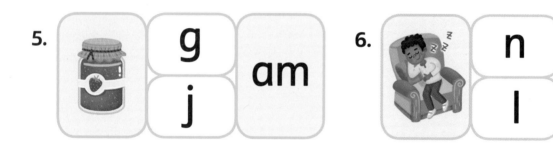 g / j **am**

6. n / l **ap**

7.  d / b **am**

8. 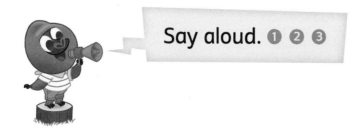 f / h **am**

Say aloud. ❶ ❷ ❸

B **Match and write.**

1.

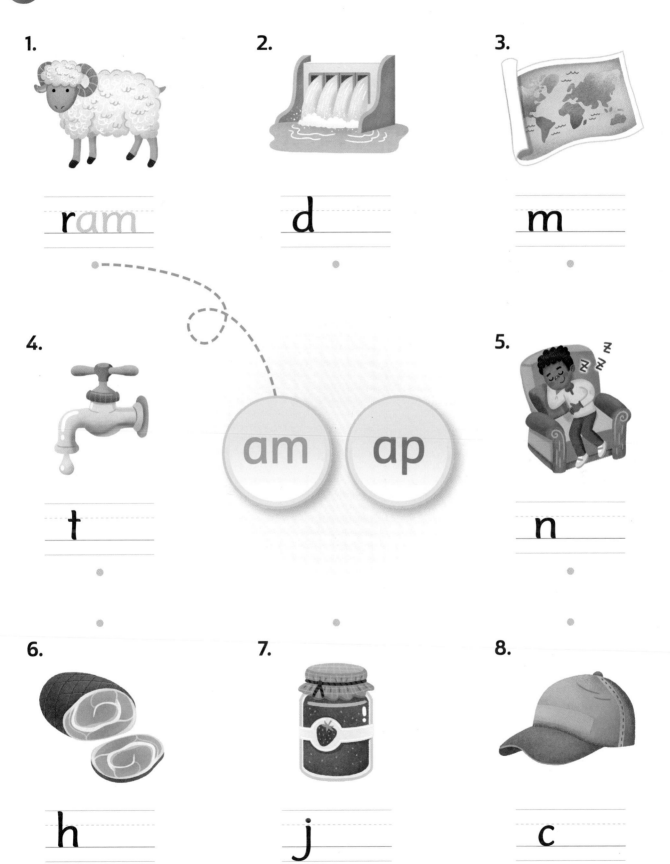

r am

2.

d

3.

m

4.

t

am   ap

5.

n

6.

h

7.

j

8.

c

A Listen and check. 🎧12

1.

2.

3.

B Listen and circle. 🎧13

1.  A (cap / tap) is on the map.

2.  A (ram / ham) is in the jam.

3.  A (nap / tap) is at the dam.

C Find and circle.

jam   cap   dam   nap

k g j a m e f c a p l m
n a p t s d a m f g n k
k s r a m t g u a m a p i k
l n t a p j n h a m

ram   map   ham   tap

● **Let's read together.** (14)

"Where is my cap?"

"Where is my jam?"

"Where is my map?"

The little ram is taking a nap.

Sight Words

where   little   taking   a

Writing Time

● **Write and say.**

1.  d + am → dam

2.   h + am → ham

3.  j + am → jam

4.  r + am → ram

5.  c + ap → cap

6.  m + ap → map

7.  n + ap → nap

8.  t + ap → tap

➡ Go to the workbook p. 6 **19**

Short Vowel e

Listen and repeat.

A **Read step by step.**

1.

e

e n

h e n

2.

e

e t

j e t

B Read and say. 🎧16

en — Ben, pen, ten

et — net, vet, wet

C Point and chant. 🎧17

en

et

A Listen and stick. 🎧18

1.

2.

3.

4.

5.

6.

7.

8.
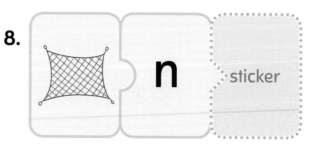

Say aloud. ❶ ❷ ❸

B **Match and write.**

1.

hen

2.

w___

3.

t___

4.

v___

en   et

5.

B___

6.

p___

7.

n___

8.

j___

Listen and check. (19)

1.  ☐  ☐  ☐

2.  ☐  ☐  ☐

3.  ☐  ☐  ☐

B **Listen and circle.** (20)

1.  Ben has a (pen / ten).

2.  A hen is (vet / wet).

3.  A ten is on the (jet / net).

C Find and circle.

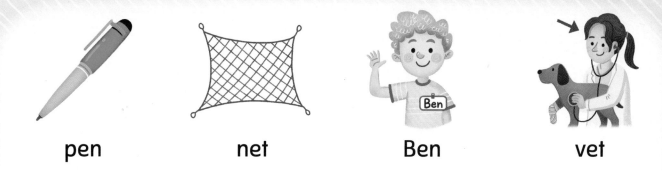

pen   net   Ben   vet

v	e	t	a	c	d	e	f
f	g	k	h	t	B	e	n
B	u	o	p	w	e	t	k
s	t	n	u	e	d	l	m
v	w	e	x	y	n	j	o
z	a	t	e	n	b	e	s
h	h	n	e	f	g	t	h

jet   hen   wet   ten

● **Let's read together.** (21)

A hen is wet.

I'm Ben.
I have a net.

Oh, let's go
to a vet.

Thank you,
Ben.

Sight Words
I'm   have   let's   go   to

Writing Time

✏️ Writing Time

● **Write and say.**

1.   h + en → hen

2.   B + en → Ben

3.   p + en → pen

4.   t + en → ten

5.   j + et → jet

6.   n + et → net

7.    v + et → vet

8.    w + et → wet

Unit 04

Short Vowel e

• **Listen and repeat.** (22)

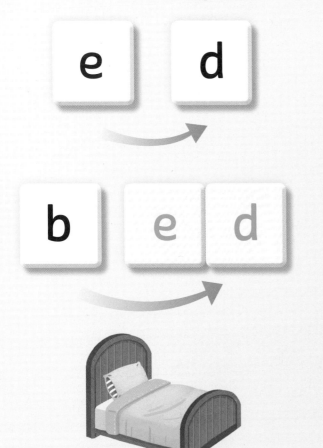

e → d

b e d

e → g

b e g

A **Read step by step.**

1.
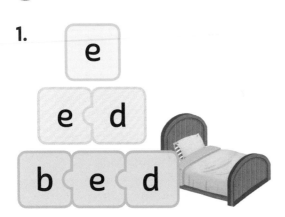

e

e d

b e d

2.

e

e g

b e g

B **Read and say.** 23

ed

red

Ted

wed

eg

keg

leg

Meg

C **Point and chant.** 24

ed

eg

A Listen and color.

1.

D
T ed

2.

c
k eg

3.

l
r ed

4.

d
b eg

5.

w
m ed

6.

r
l eg

7.

d
b ed

8.

M
W eg

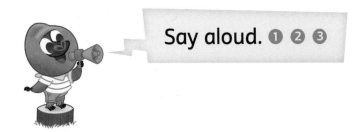 Say aloud. ① ② ③

B **Match and write.**

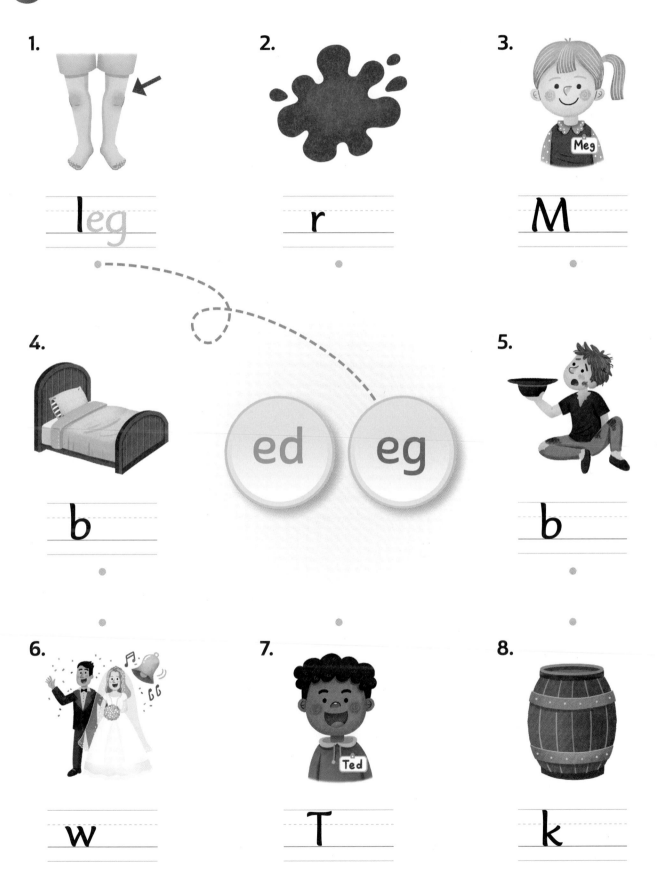

1.

leg

2.

r

3.

M

4.

b

ed   eg

5.

b

6.

w

7.

T

8.

k

A Listen and check. 26

1.

2.

3.

B Listen and circle. 27

1.  Ted and Meg (wed / red).

2.  The apple is on the (bed / keg).

3.  The (keg / leg) is red.

C Find and circle.

beg   Ted   keg   wed

k d o b e g p q T e d s
z y i w e d t u k e g r s
u k r e d g r l e g s m l n
d p b e d o j M e g

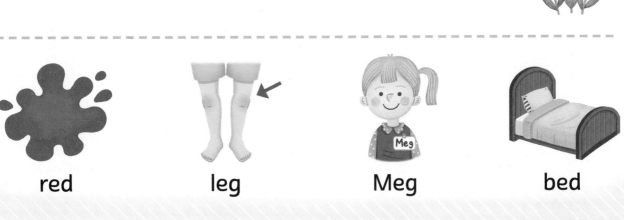

red   leg   Meg   bed

● **Let's read together.** 28

"Who are you?"
"I'm Ted."

"Ted, you got red."

"Oh, I have a leg!"

Hi, Mom!

Hi, Ted!

Sight Words

who   got   hi   Mom

● **Write and say.**

1.  b + ed ➡ bed

2.  r + ed ➡ red

3.  T + ed ➡ Ted

4.  w + ed ➡ wed

5.  b + eg ➡ beg

6. k + eg ➡ keg

7. l + eg ➡ leg

8.  M + eg ➡ Meg

➡ Go to the workbook p. 14

Short Vowel i

● **Listen and repeat.** (29)

i g → b i g

i d → k i d

i p → d i p

A **Read step by step.**

1.
i

i g

b i g

2.
i

i d

k i d

3.
i

i p

d i p

B Read and say. 30

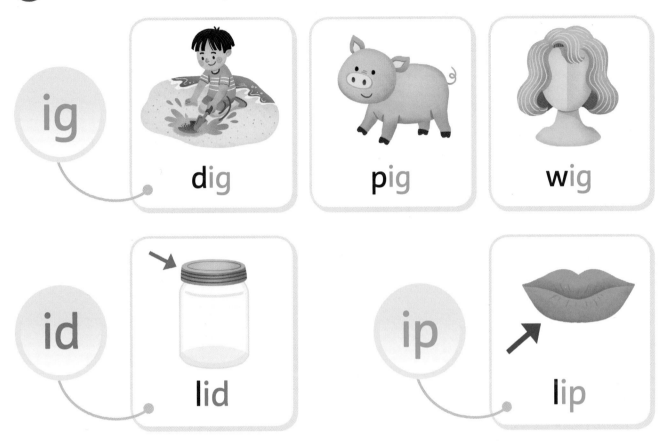

C Point and chant. 31

Listen and stick. 🎧 32

1.

2.

3.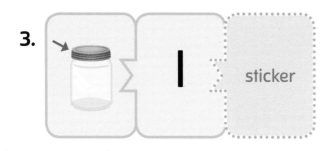

4.

5.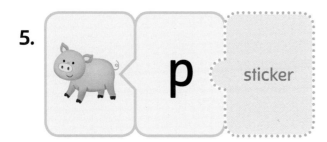

6.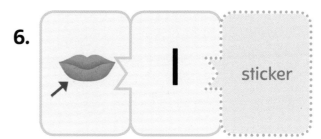

7.

8.

Say aloud. ❶ ❷ ❸

B Match and write.

1.

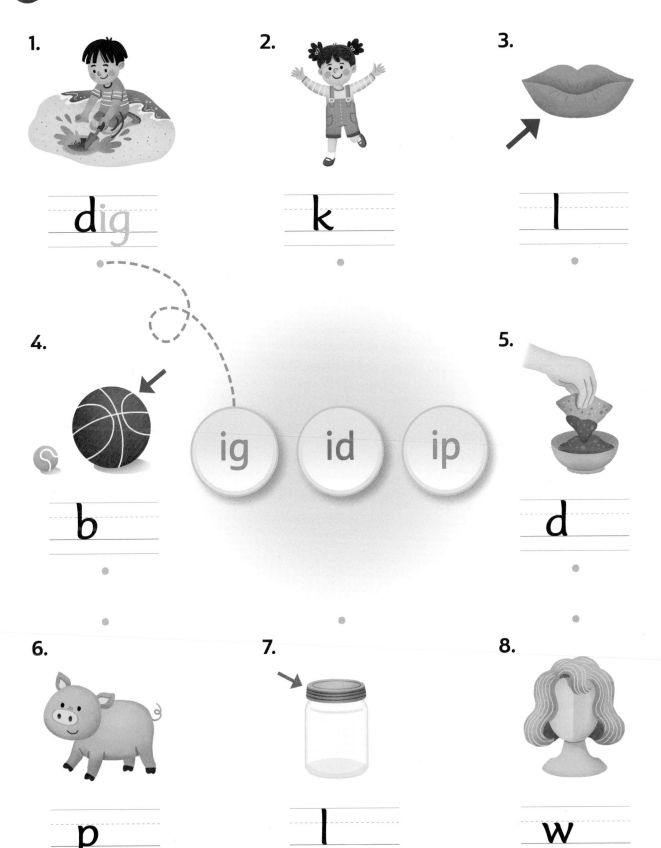

d**ig**

2.

k

3.

l

4.

b

ig   id   ip

5.

d

6.

p

7.

l

8.

w

A Listen and check. 33

1.  ☐  ☐  ☐

2.  ☐  ☐  ☐

3.  ☐  ☐  ☐

B Listen and circle. 34

1.    This pig is very (big / dig).

2.    The kid opens the (lip / lid).

3.    I have a funny (wig / pig).

C Find and circle.

lip   pig   kid   big

dig   lid   dip   wig

● **Let's read together.** 🎧35

Dig, dig, dig!
The kid opens the lid.

"It's a wig.
I don't like it."

Sight Words

opens   don't   like   it

"Oh, I like it!"

Writing Time

Write and say.

1.  b + ig → big

2.  d + ig → dig

3.  p + ig → pig

4.  w + ig → wig

5.  k + id → kid

6.   l + id → lid

7.  d + ip → dip

8.   l + ip → lip

A Listen and match. (36)

1.   2.   3.   4.

at   an   am   ap

5.   6.   7.   8.

B Look and number.

1. hen ☐2   2. pig ☐   3. tap ☐   4. kid ☐

C Read and write.

| jet | red | leg | bed |
| dig | vet | lid | ten |

1. dig

2.

3.

4.

5.

6.

7.

8.

D Listen and color. (37)

1.

c — ap / et

2.

w — et / ig

3.

p — et / en

4.

h — am / eg

5.

m — an / ed

6.

w — ed / an

7.

b — ap / at

8.

k — eg / ip

E Choose and write.

i   a̶   e

1.

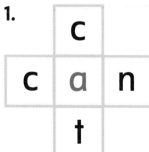

```
    c
c   a   n
    t
```

2.

```
    b
w       g
    g
```

3.

```
    k
b       g
    g
```

F **Look and write.**

hen	dig	kid	pig
lid	~~dip~~	lip	ten

-ip

dip

-en

-id

-ig

● **Listen and repeat.** 38

| i | n | → | i | t | → | i | x |

| b | i | n | → | h | i | t | → | f | i | x |

A **Read step by step.**

1.

i

i n

b i n

2.
i

i t

h i t

3.
i

i x

f i x

B Read and say. 39

C Point and chant. 40

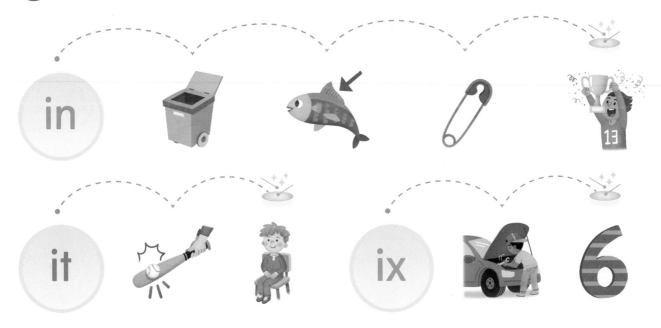

A **Listen and color.** 41

1.
p
f
in

2.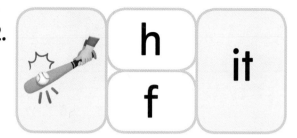
h
f
it

3.
s
z
ix

4.
d
b
in

5.
w
m
in

6.
p
f
ix

7.
c
s
it

8.
b
p
in

 Say aloud. ❶ ❷ ❸

B **Match and write.**

1.

fix

2.

s

3.

b

4.

h

in   it   ix

5.

w

6.

f

7.

p

8.

s

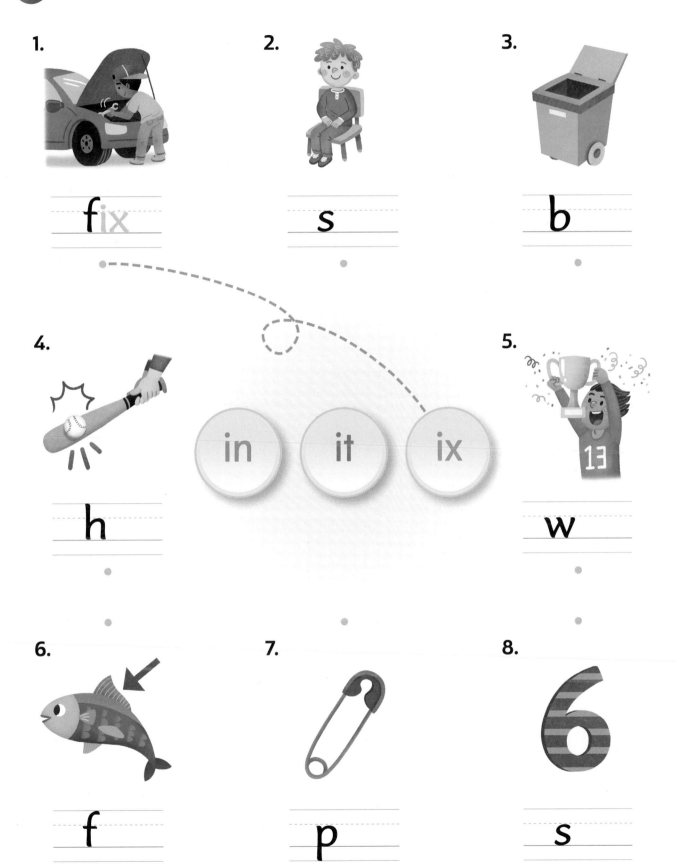

A Listen and check. 🎧42

1.  ☐  ☐  ☐

2.  ☐  ☐  ☐

3.  ☐  ☐  ☐

B Listen and circle. 🎧43

1.    There are six (bins / pins).

2.    The pin sits on the (fin / win).

3.    I (sit / hit) the bin.

C **Find and circle.**

win   bin   six   sit

m	b	i	n	g	b	t	h
a	e	f	h	i	t	j	u
b	l	m	p	a	s	i	t
s	n	w	o	f	i	x	h
i	s	t	i	u	v	a	f
x	b	c	d	n	e	f	i
c	p	i	n	g	h	c	n

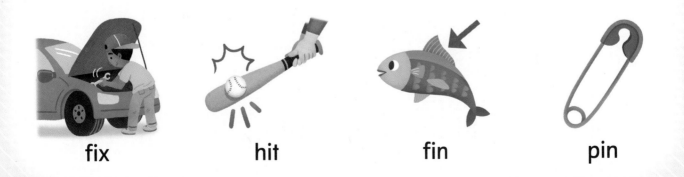

fix   hit   fin   pin

Story Time

● **Let's read together.** 44

Look at the fin.

The fin hits the boat.

He has six apples.

I'm sorry.

Sight Words

look　at　he　has　sorry

● **Write and say.**

1. b + in → bin

2.  f + in → fin

3.  p + in → pin

4.  w + in → win

5.  h + it → hit

6.  s + it → sit

7. f + ix → fix

8. s + ix → six

Short Vowel O

Listen and repeat. 45

o → p

h op → p

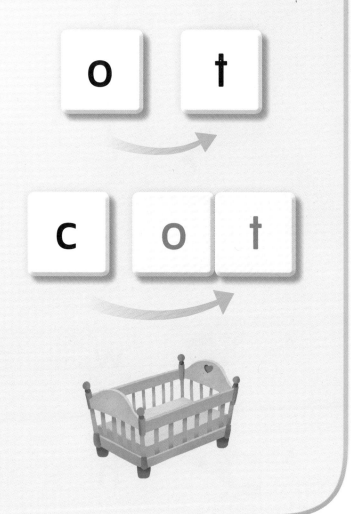

o → t

c ot → t

A **Read step by step.**

1.

o

o p

h o p

2.
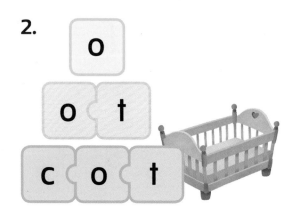

o

o t

c o t

B Read and say. 🎧46

op — mop · pop · top

ot — dot · hot · pot

C Point and chant. 🎧47

op

ot

A Listen and stick. 48

1.  t op

2.  c sticker

3.  m sticker

4.  p sticker

5.  p sticker

6.  h sticker

7. 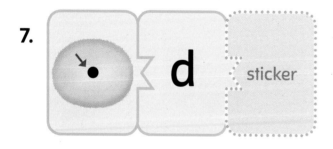 d sticker

8.  h sticker

 Say aloud. ❶ ❷ ❸

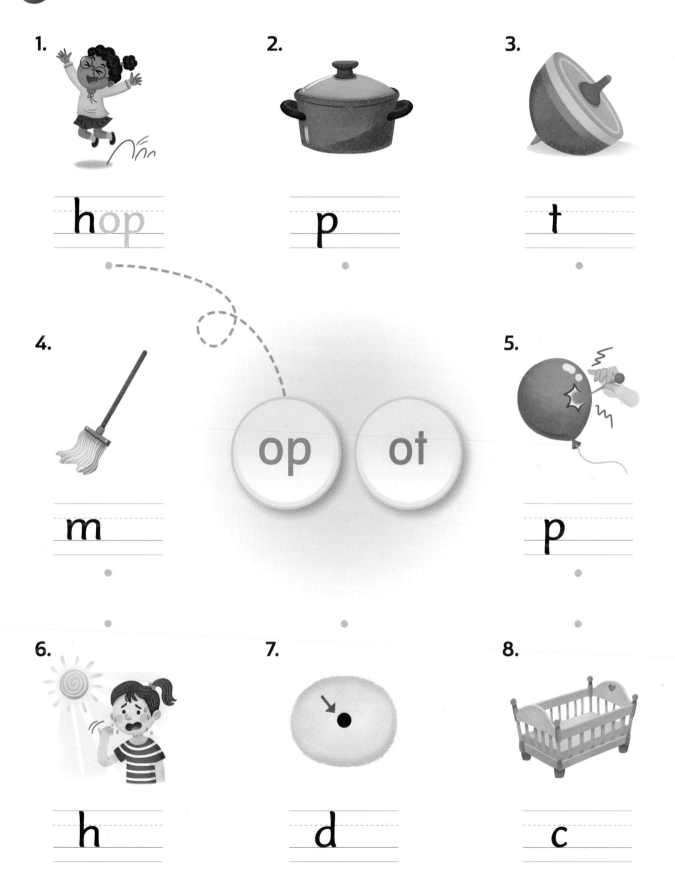

B **Match and write.**

1.

hop

2.

p

3.

t

op   ot

4.

m

5.

p

6.

h

7.

d

8.

c

A Listen and check. 49

1.

2.

3.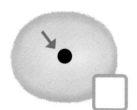

B Listen and circle. 50

1.  The pot is (hot / hop).

2.  She hops on the (dot / cot).

3.  The (mop / top) is next to the cot.

C Find and circle.

pop   top   hot   dot

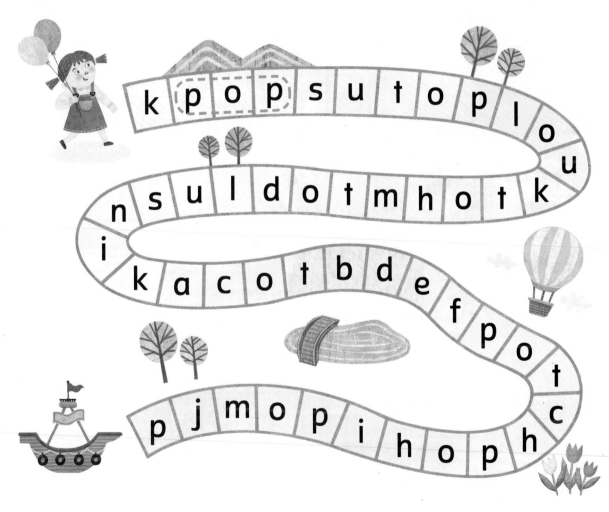

k p o p s u t o p l o u

n s u l d o t m h o t k

i

k a c o t b d e f p o t c

p j m o p i h o p h

cot   pot   hop   mop

Story Time

● **Let's read together.** 51

A top is hopping.
Hop, hop, hop!

The top hops into the pot.

"Oh, it's hot."

The top turns into a mop.

Sight Words

the   into   it's   turns

● **Write and say.**

1.   h + op → hop

2.   m + op → mop

3. 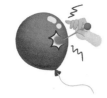   p + op → pop

4.   t + op → top

5.    c + ot → cot

6.   d + ot → dot

7.   h + ot → hot

8.    p + ot → pot

Short Vowel O

● **Listen and repeat.** 🎧52

| o | g | | o | d | | o | x |

| d | o | g | | n | o | d | | b | o | x |

  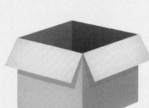

A **Read step by step.**

1.
| o |
| o | g |
| d | o | g |

2.
| o |
| o | d |
| n | o | d |

3.
| o |
| o | x |
| b | o | x |

B Read and say. 53

og — fog | jog | log

od — rod

ox — fox

C Point and chant. 54

A **Listen and color.** 55

1.
f
p
ox

2.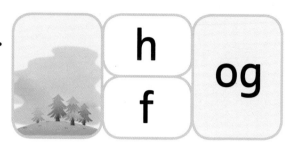
h
f
og

3.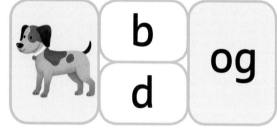
b
d
og

4.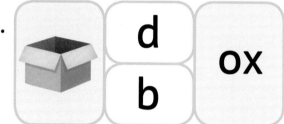
d
b
ox

5.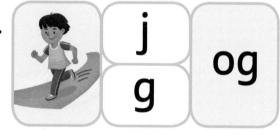
j
g
og

6.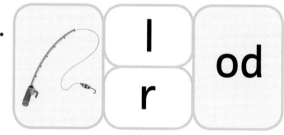
l
r
od

7.
n
l
og

8.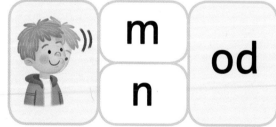
m
n
od

 Say aloud. ❶ ❷ ❸

B Match and write.

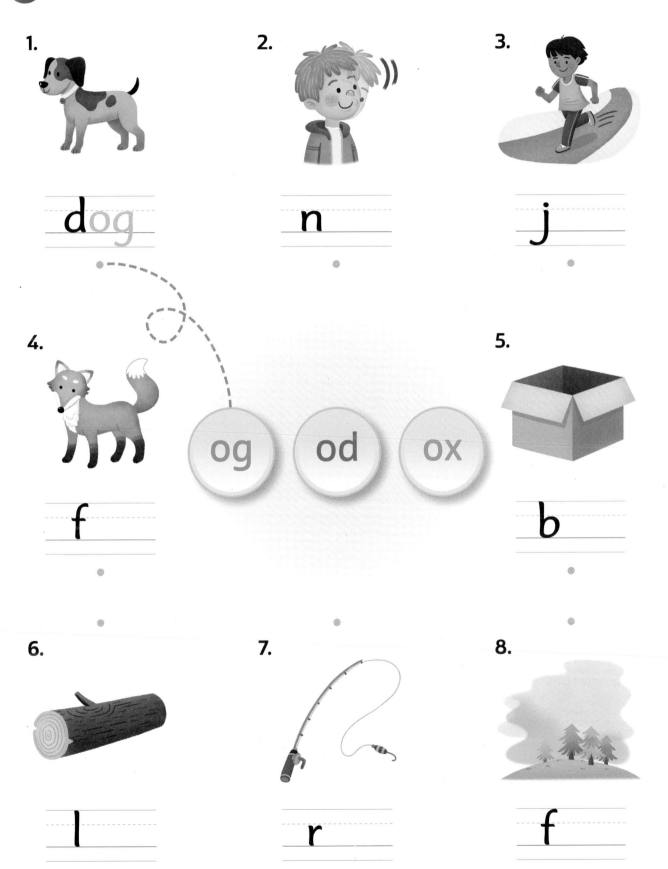

1.

d og

2.

n

3.

j

4.

f

og   od   ox

5.

b

6.

l

7.

r

8.

f

A Listen and check. 56

1.

2.

3.
 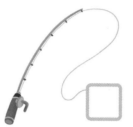 

B Listen and circle. 57

1.  The dog is in the (box / fox).

2.  The fox sits on a (log / fog).

3.  The dog has a (nod / rod).

C Find and circle.

box   dog   log   nod

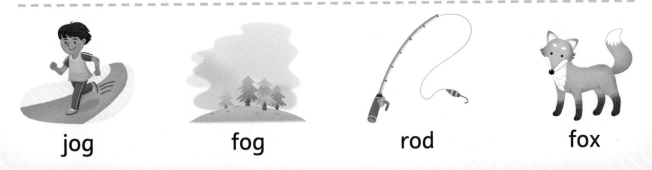

jog   fog   rod   fox

● **Let's read together.** 58

The dog walks on the log.

The fox walks on the log.

The dog and the fox are in the fog.

The dog and the fox are under the log.

Sight Words

walks   on   and   under

Writing Time

● **Write and say.**

1. d + og ➡ dog

2.  f + og ➡ fog

3.  j + og ➡ jog

4.  l + og ➡ log

5.  n + od ➡ nod

6. r + od ➡ rod

7. b + ox ➡ box

8. f + ox ➡ fox

Short Vowel **u**

● **Listen and repeat.** 59

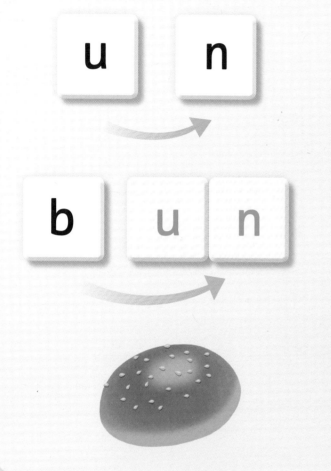

A Read step by step.

1.

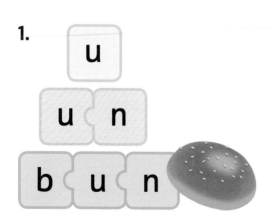

2.

B **Read and say.** 🎧60

un

fun

run

sun

ug

bug

hug

rug

C **Point and chant.** 🎧61

un

ug

A Listen and stick. (62)

1.

2.

3.

4.

5.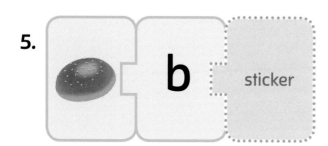

6.

7.

8.

Say aloud. ❶ ❷ ❸

B Match and write.

1.

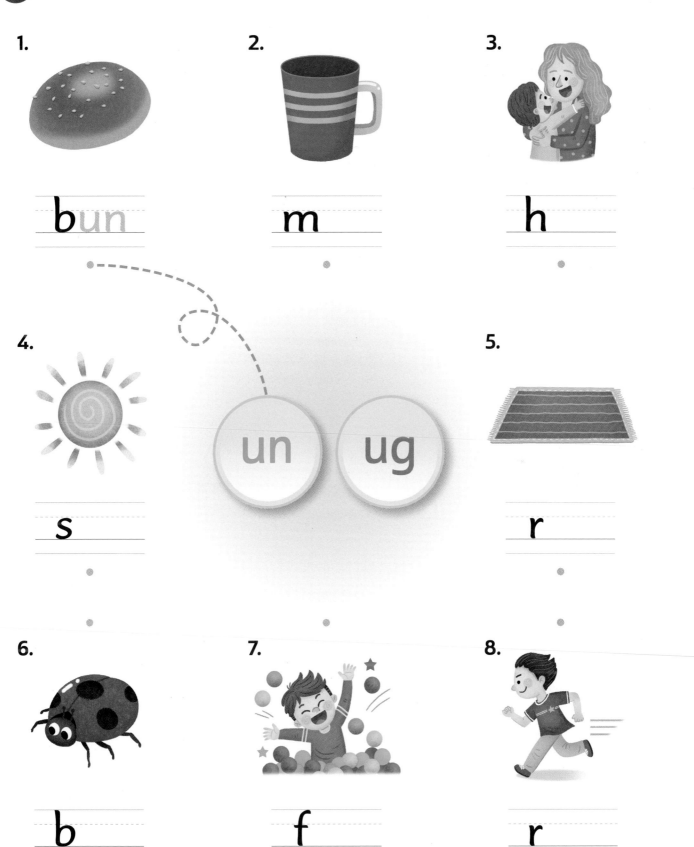

bun

2.

m

3.

h

4.

s

un   ug

5.

r

6.

b

7.

f

8.

r

Listen and check.

1.

2.

3.

B **Listen and circle.** 64

1.

The bug is on the (bun / sun).

2.

The sun is (fun / run).

3.

The (mug / hug) is on the rug.

C **Find and circle.**

mug

bun

bug

run

z	x	b	u	n	a	b	s
c	b	u	g	s	r	h	u
i	j	k	m	m	u	n	n
o	p	m	q	u	n	r	s
t	f	u	n	u	g	y	r
u	a	c	d	g	e	g	u
h	h	u	g	k	m	o	q	g

hug

fun

rug

sun

 **Story Time**

● **Let's read together.** 🎧65

The bug sees a bun.

The bug runs.

The bug falls into the mug.

It's fun.

Sight Words
sees   falls   into

Write and say.

1. b + un → bun

2.  f + un → fun

3.  r + un → run

4.  s + un → sun

5. m + ug → mug

6. b + ug → bug

7.  h + ug → hug

8.  r + ug → rug

➡ Go to the workbook p. 36

Short Vowel u

● **Listen and repeat.** 66

s

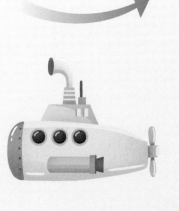

c

h

A **Read step by step.**

1. u

ub

s u b

2. u

up

c u p

3. u

ut

h u t

B Read and say. 🎧67

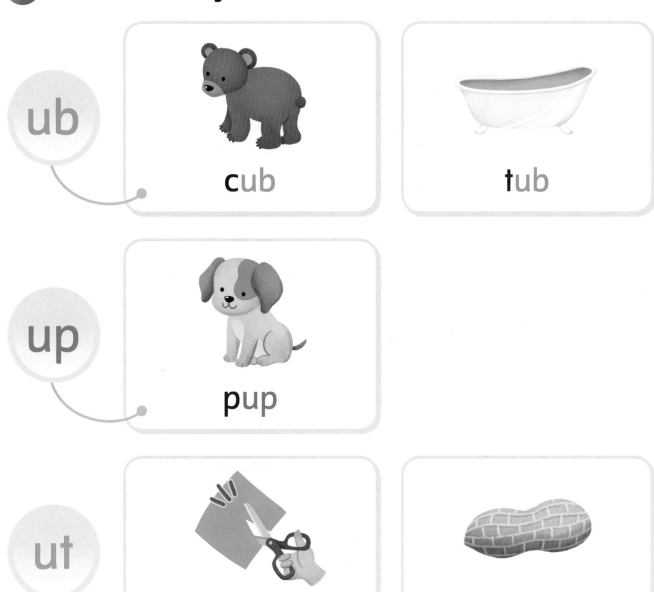

ub

cub

tub

up

pup

ut

cut

nut

C Point and chant. 🎧68

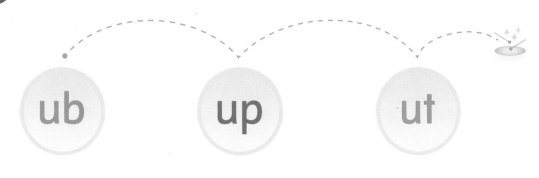

ub   up   ut

24000

 A **Listen and color.** 69

1. 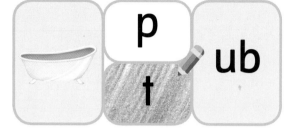 p / t | ub

2. 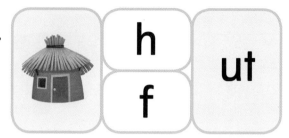 h / f | ut

3. 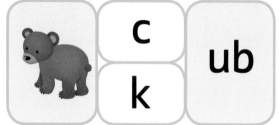 c / k | ub

4. 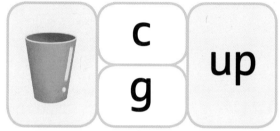 c / g | up

5. 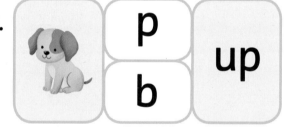 p / b | up

6.  k / c | ut

7. 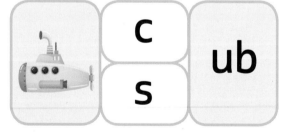 c / s | ub

8. 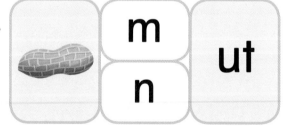 m / n | ut

 Say aloud. ① ② ③

B Match and write.

1.
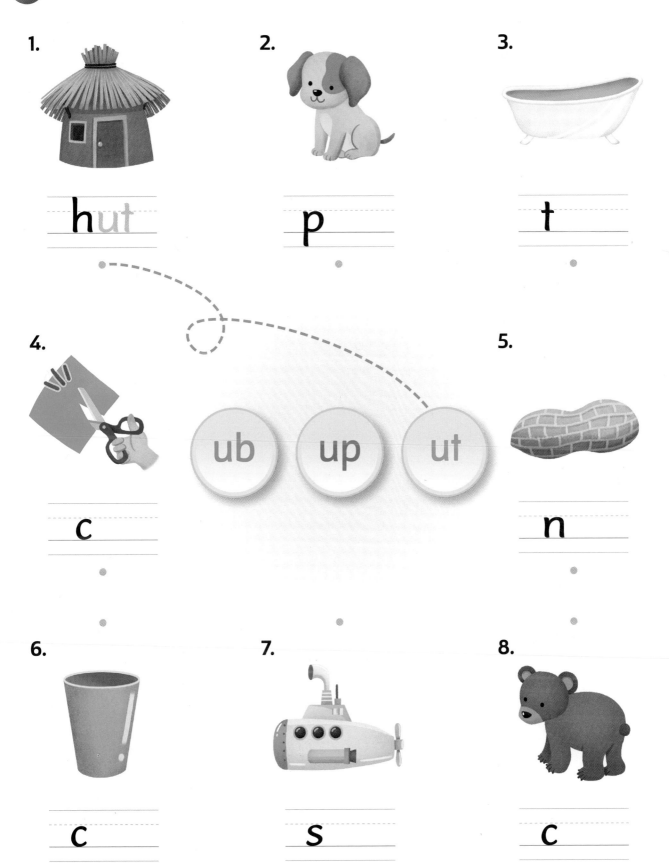
hut

2.
p

3.
t

4.
c

ub up ut

5.
n

6.
c

7.
s

8.
c

A **Listen and check.** 🎧70

1.

2.

3.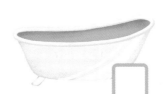

B **Listen and circle.** 🎧71

1.  The cub is in the (tub / pup).

2.  I cut the (nut / hut).

3.  The (pup / cup) is in the sub.

C Find and circle.

| cup | pup | tub | nut |

s u c u p l p u p k t p
m n u t r s g l t u b u
l c u t y u c u b a c d f h
l k h u t j i s u b

| cut | cub | sub | hut |

 **Story Time**

The tub is in the hut.

The cup is in the tub.

The pup is in the cup.

The pup eats a nut.

Sight Words

the   is   in   eats

✏ Writing Time

● **Write and say.**

1.  s + ub ➡ sub

2.   c + ub ➡ cub

3.  t + ub ➡ tub

4.   c + up ➡ cup

5.   p + up ➡ pup

6.   h + ut ➡ hut

7.  c + ut ➡ cut

8.   n + ut ➡ nut

➡ Go to the workbook p. 40 **87**

Review 2

A Listen and match. (73)

1. 2. 3. 4.

in   op   ot   it

5. 6. 7. 8.

B Look and number.

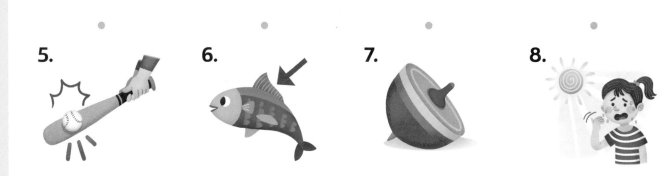

1. dot [4]   2. pop [ ]   3. pin [ ]   4. bug [ ]

C Read and write.

~~cub~~	rod	fix	mug
box	jog	win	bun

1.

cub

2.

3.

4.

5.

6.

7.

8.

D Listen and color. 74

1.

s — ix / ox

2.

h — op / un

3.

p — og / ot

4.

s — ug / un

5.

c — up / od

6.

w — in / it

7.

p — ug / up

8.

h — it / ix

E Choose and write.

i   u   ~~o~~

1.

b
f o x
x

2.

h
n t
t

3.

p
f n
n

F Look and write.

hug   dog   nod   rod

sub   fog   rug   tub

-og

dog

-od

-ub

-ug

Phonics Words

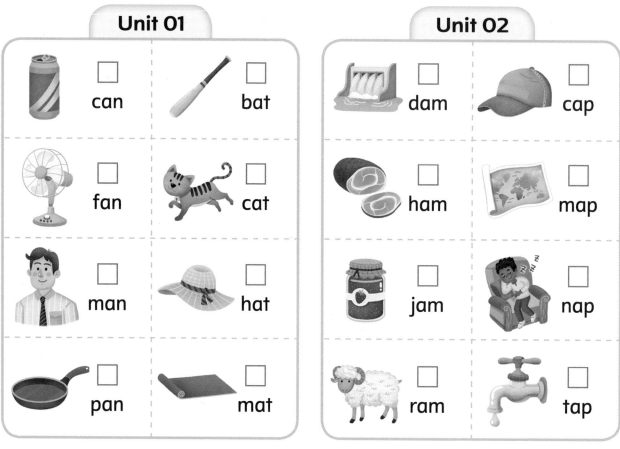

Unit 01

☐ can	☐ bat
☐ fan	☐ cat
☐ man	☐ hat
☐ pan	☐ mat

Unit 02

☐ dam	☐ cap
☐ ham	☐ map
☐ jam	☐ nap
☐ ram	☐ tap

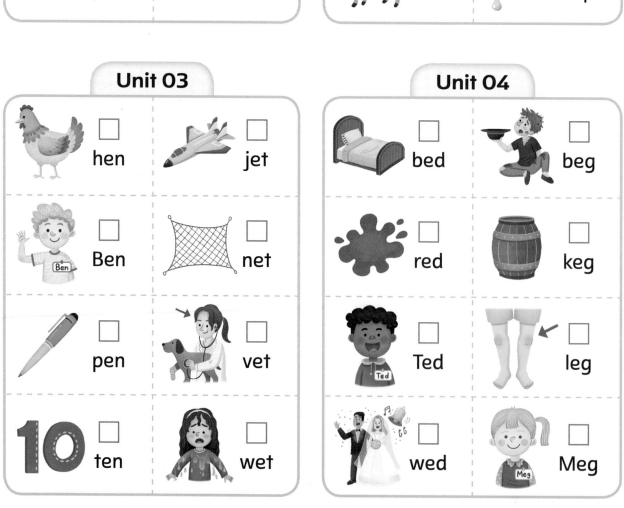

Unit 03

☐ hen	☐ jet
☐ Ben	☐ net
☐ pen	☐ vet
☐ ten	☐ wet

Unit 04

☐ bed	☐ beg
☐ red	☐ keg
☐ Ted	☐ leg
☐ wed	☐ Meg

Unit 05

big ☐   kid ☐

dig ☐   lid ☐

pig ☐   dip ☐

wig ☐   lip ☐

Unit 06

bin ☐   hit ☐

fin ☐   sit ☐

pin ☐   fix ☐

win ☐   six ☐

Unit 07

hop ☐   cot ☐

mop ☐   dot ☐

pop ☐   hot ☐

top ☐   pot ☐

Unit 08

dog ☐   nod ☐

fog ☐   rod ☐

jog ☐   box ☐

log ☐   fox ☐

Unit 09

bun ☐	mug ☐
fun ☐	bug ☐
run ☐	hug ☐
sun ☐	rug ☐

Unit 10

sub ☐	pup ☐
cub ☐	hut ☐
tub ☐	cut ☐
cup ☐	nut ☐

• Sight Words

Unit 01	the	is	on	my	
Unit 02	where	little	taking	a	
Unit 03	I'm	have	let's	go	to
Unit 04	who	got	hi	Mom	
Unit 05	opens	don't	like	it	
Unit 06	look	at	he	has	sorry
Unit 07	the	into	it's	turns	
Unit 08	walks	on	and	under	
Unit 09	sees	falls	into		
Unit 10	the	is	in	eats	

Let's Go to the English World
Phonics

Readers 2

The Magic Pen

The cat has a magic pen.

The cat is wet.

"I can make a fan!"

The cat has ham.

The cat doesn't have a pan.

It is time for bed.

"I can make a bed!"

"Ouch, my leg!"

The Dot Story

We're just dots.

I sit in a pot.

The pot is hot.

I hop into the pan.

I'm on the egg.

The kid has ink.

I'm under the ink.

Now, we're not just dots.

Put Them Here! (77)

The cub has a rod.

 Oops, it is a mug!

The pup is in the sub.

The pup sees a box and a can.

Put them here! He nods.

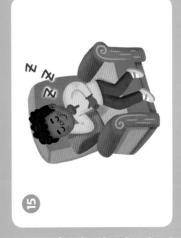

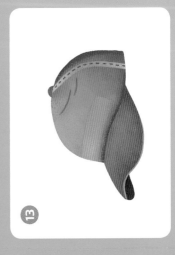

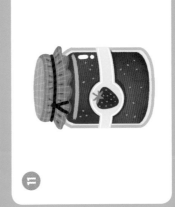

tap	ram	mat	pan
nap	jam	hat	man
map	ham	cat	fan
cap	dam	bat	can

20

24

28

32

19

23

27

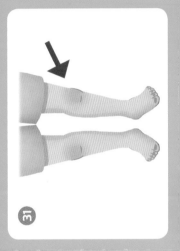

31

18

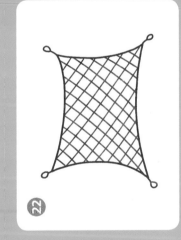

22

26

30

17

21

25

29

Meg	wed	wet	ten
leg	Ted	vet	pen
keg	red	net	Ben
beg	bed	jet	hen

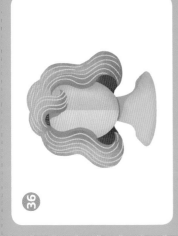
36

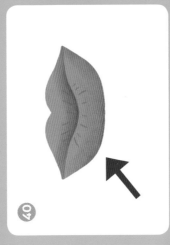
40

44

48

35

39

43

47

34

38

42

46

33

37

41

45

six	win	lip	wig
fix	pin	dip	pig
sit	fin	lid	dig
hit	bin	kid	big

52

56

60

64

51

55

59

63

50

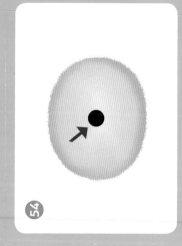

54

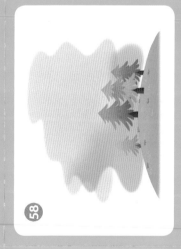

58

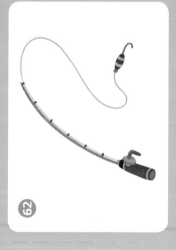

62

49

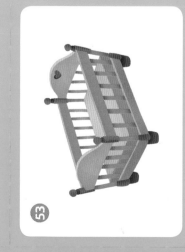

53

57

61

fox	log	pot	top
box	jog	hot	pop
rod	fog	dot	mop
nod	dog	cot	hop

68

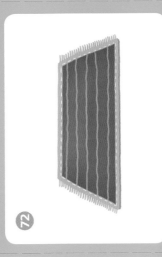

72

76

80

67

71

75

79

66

70

74

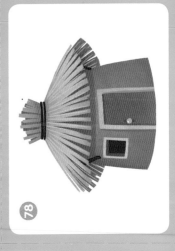

78

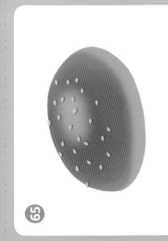

65

69

73

77

nut	cup	rug	sun
cut	tub	hug	run
hut	cub	bug	fun
pup	sub	mug	bun

Congratulations!

Let's Go to the English World

Phonics ❷ Short Vowels

The certificate is presented to

_____ .

Signature _____

Date _____

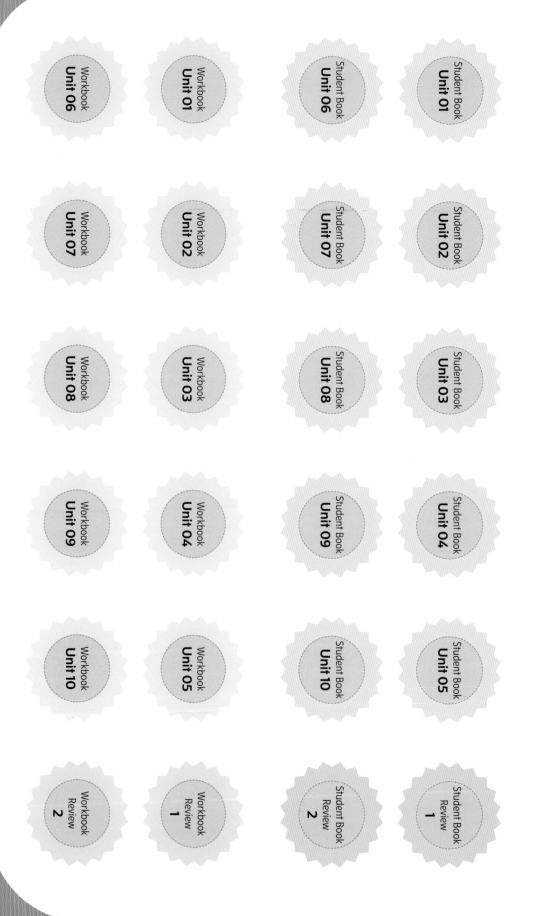

Sticker Chart

Unit 01 p. 6

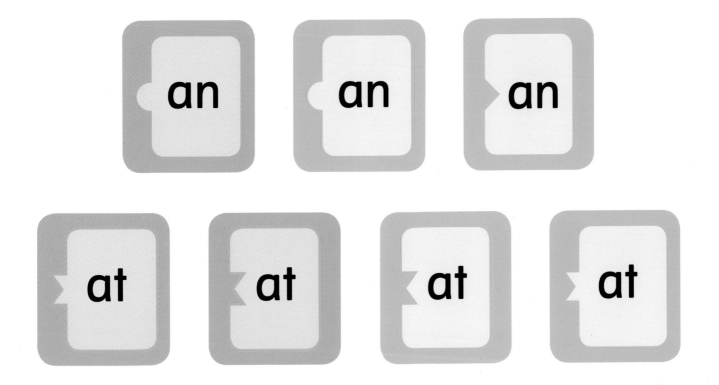

Unit 03 p. 22

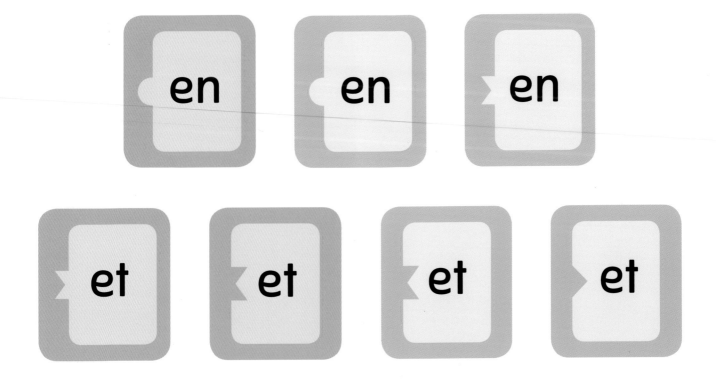

Unit 05   p. 38

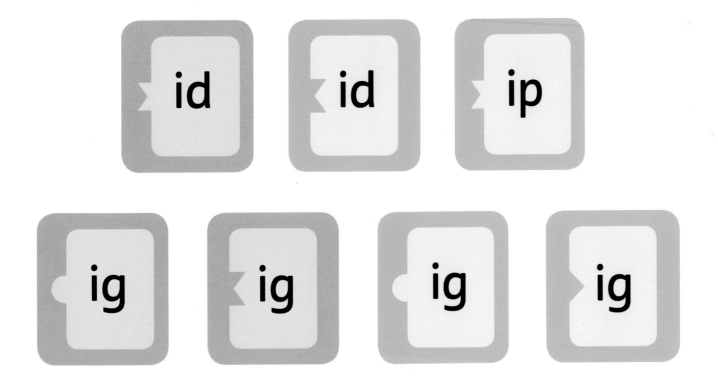

Unit 07   p. 58

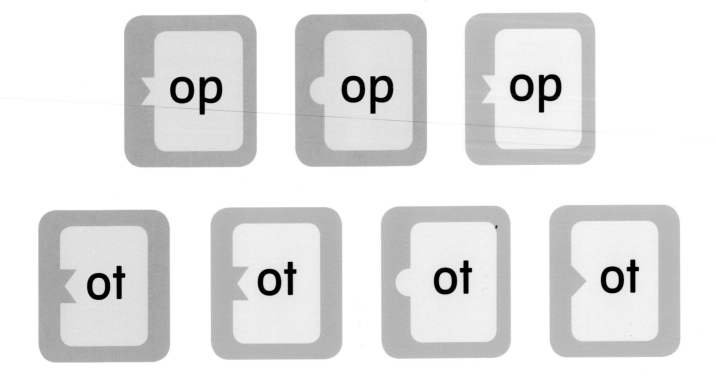

Unit 09 p. 74

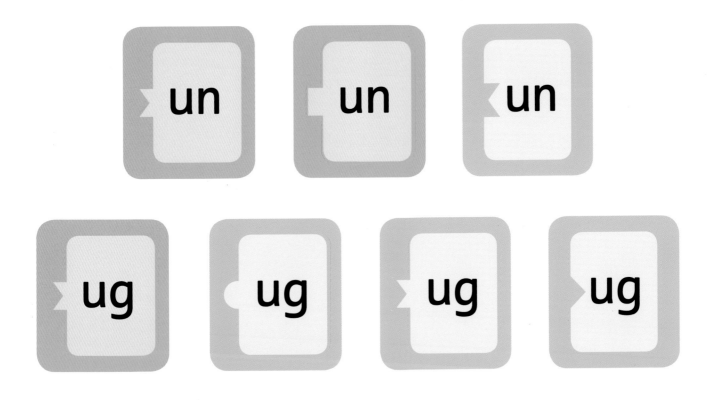

Praise Stickers

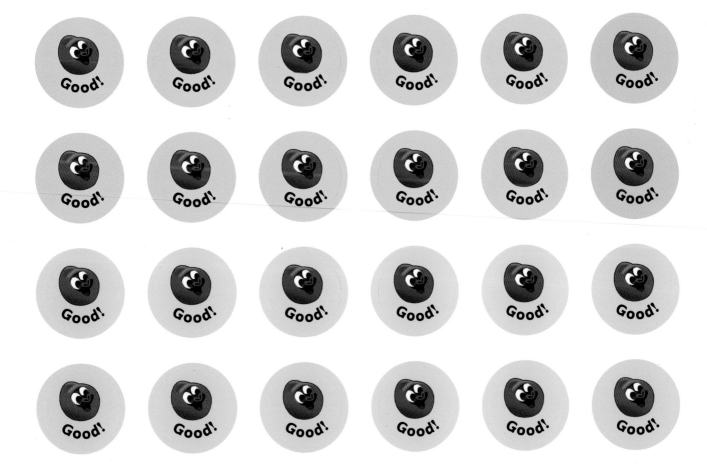

LET'S GO

to the English World

2nd Edition

2

WORKBOOK

Phonics

Short Vowels

CHUNJAE EDUCATION, INC.

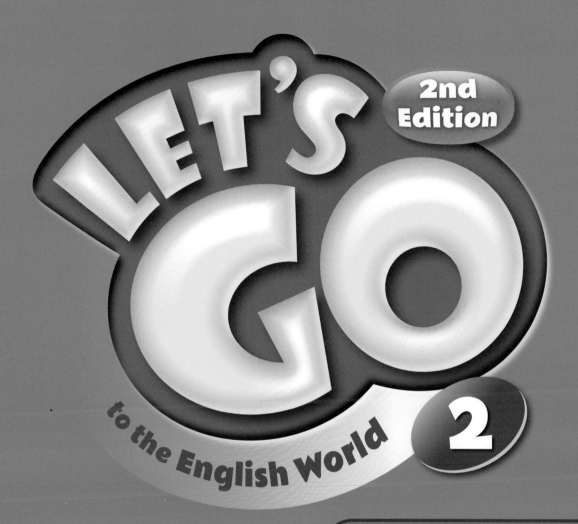

LET'S GO

2nd Edition

to the English World

2

WORKBOOK

Phonics

CHUNJAE EDUCATION, INC.

Short Vowels

A Look and match.

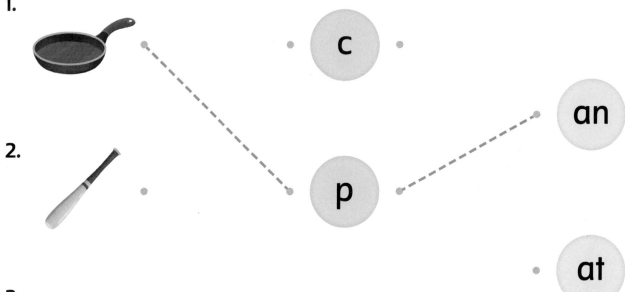

1.

2.

3.

c

p

b

an

at

B Read and circle.

1.

hat
cat
mat

2.

can
bat
man

3.

fan
man
can

4.

man
mat
cat

C Say and choose.

1.

an

☑   ☐   ☑

2.

at

☐   ☐   ☐

D Unscramble and write.

1.

f n a

fan

2.

a t h

_____

3.

b t a

_____

4.

n a c

_____

E **Choose and write.**

an	at

1.

c an

2.

p

3.

c

4.

m

5.

f

6.

h

7.

b

8.

m

F Read and number.

 **1**
 **2**
 **3**

1. A can is in the pan.   `3`

2. A cat is on the mat.

3. A hat is on the man.

G Read and trace.

1.  A _cat_ is on the _mat_ .

2.  A _can_ is in the _pan_ .

3.  A _hat_ is on the _man_ .

Short Vowel a

A Look and match.

1.

2.

3.

h

d

c

am

ap

B Read and circle.

1.

nap

ram

map

2.

tap

ram

ham

3.

jam

dam

nap

4.

nap

tap

cap

C Say and choose.

1.

am

2.

ap

D Unscramble and write.

1.  n p a

_____

2.  r m a

_____

3.  a d m

_____

4.  p m a

_____

E Choose and write.

am   ap

1.
h

2.
c

3.
n

4.
d

5.
m

6.
j

7.
r

8.
t

F Read and number.

1    **2**    **3**

1. A cap is on the map. ☐

2. A ram is in the jam. ☐

3. A tap is at the dam. ☐

G Read and trace.

1.    A ___cap___ is on the ___map___ .

2.    A ___ram___ is in the ___jam___ .

3.    A ___tap___ is at the ___dam___ .

A Look and match.

1.

2.

3.
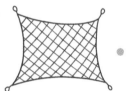

p

n

j

en

et

B Read and circle.

1.

ten

hen

vet

2.

jet

vet

pen

3.

vet

pen

wet

4.

10

ten

Ben

net

C Say and choose.

1.

en

 ☐    ☐    ☐

2.

et

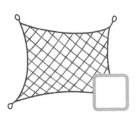 ☐    ☐    ☐

D Unscramble and write.

1.  t n e

_____

2.  e t v

_____

3.  n e p

_____

4. e w t

_____

en	et

1.

j

2.

B

3.
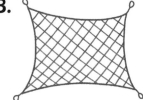

n

4.

t

5.

w

6.

p

7.

h

8.

v

F **Read and number.**

1  2  3

1. Ben has a pen. ☐

2. A hen is wet. ☐

3. A ten is on the jet. ☐

G **Read and trace.**

1.    Ben has a pen .

2.    A hen is wet .

3.    A ten is on the jet .

A Look and match.

1.

l

ed

2.

r

eg

3.

b

B Read and circle.

1.

beg
leg
bed

2.

red
wed
leg

3.

keg
beg
bed

4.

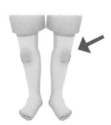

red
leg
keg

C **Say and choose.**

1. **ed**

2. **eg**

D **Unscramble and write.**

1.
   e g b

   _____

2. e g k

   _____

3. d e w

   _____

4. d r e

   _____

E **Choose and write.**

ed   eg

1.

b_____

2.

T_____

3.
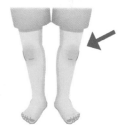

l_____

4.

M_____

5.

r_____

6.

b_____

7.

w_____

8.

k_____

F Read and number.

 1    2    3

1.   Ted and Meg wed.   ☐

2.   The apple is on the bed.   ☐

3.   The keg is red.   ☐

G Read and trace.

1.     Ted and Meg wed .

2.    The apple is on the bed .

3.     The keg is red .

A Look and match.

1.
 • • d • • ig

2.
 • • k • • id

3.
 • • b • • ip

B Read and circle.

1.

kid
dig
pig

2.

lid
lip
kid

3.

dig
wig
dip

4.

lid
dip
lip

C Say and choose.

1. **ig**

2. **id**

3. **ip**

D Unscramble and write.

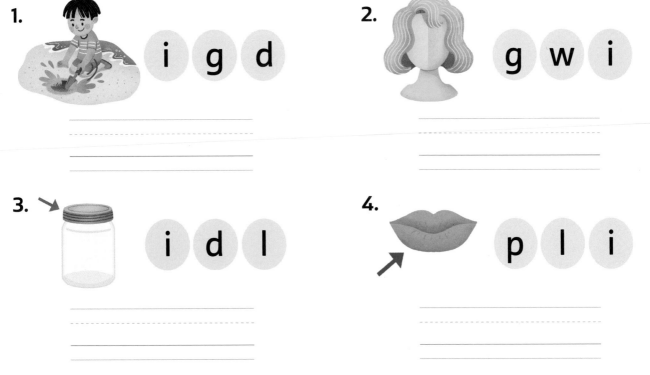

1. i g d

2. g w i

3. i d l

4. p l i

E Choose and write.

ig	id	ip

1.

p ___

2.

k ___

3.

l ___

4.

b ___

5.

d ___

6.

w ___

7.

d ___

8.

l ___

F Read and number.

1.   This pig is very big. ☐

2.   I have a funny wig. ☐

3.   The kid opens the lid. ☐

G Read and trace.

1.   This _pig_ is very _big_ .

2.   The _kid_ opens the _lid_ .

3.   I have a funny _wig_ .

Review 1

A Look and circle.

1. **ig**

2. **ap**

3. **ed**

4. **an**
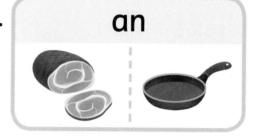

5. **et**
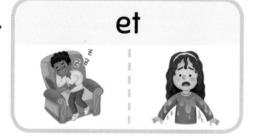

6. **ip**
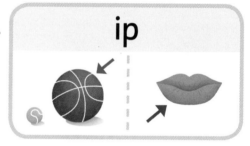

B Write and say.

1.

c_a_n

2.

li__

3.

__et

4.

__ap

5.

j__t

6.

ta__

C Look and write.

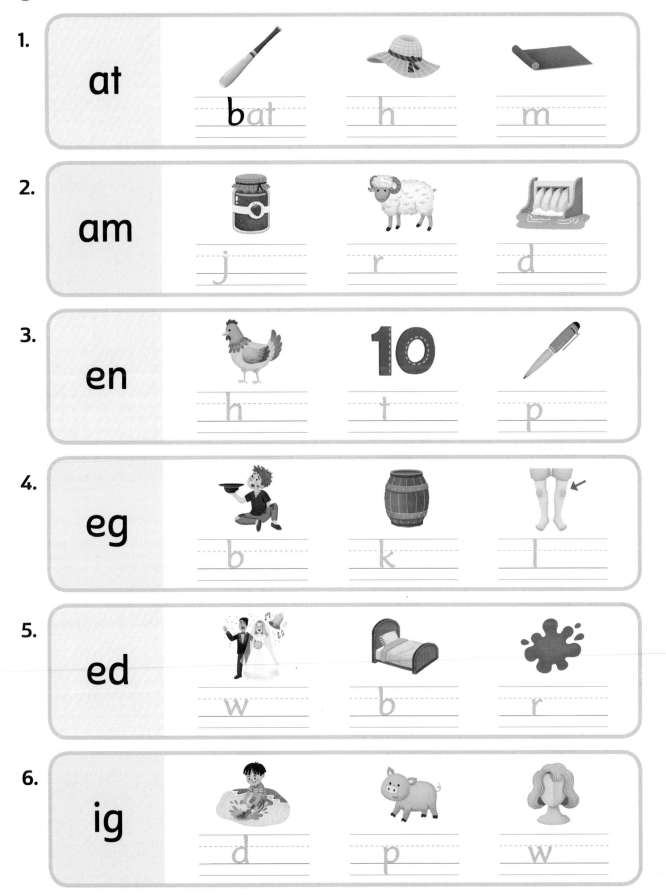

1. **at**
   b at   h   m

2. **am**
   j   r   d

3. **en**
   h   t   p

4. **eg**
   b   k   l

5. **ed**
   w   b   r

6. **ig**
   d   p   w

Short Vowel i

A Look and match.

1.

•   • h •   • in

2.

•   • f •   • it

3.

•   • b •   • ix

B Read and circle.

1.

fin
fix
sit

2.

win
pin
fix

3.

pin
fin
hit

4.

sit
fix
six

C Say and choose.

1. in

2. it

3. ix

D Unscramble and write.

1. f n i

2. n b i

3. i t h

4. i x f

E Choose and write.

in	it	ix

1.

_s_ ____

2.

_p_ ____

3.

_h_ ____

4.

_s_ ____

5.

_b_ ____

6.

_w_ ____

7.

_f_ ____

8.

_f_ ____

F Read and number.

1  **2**  **3**

1. I hit the bin.

2. The pin sits on the fin.

3. There are six bins.

G Read and trace.

1.  There are ___six___ ___bins___ .

2.  The ___pin___ ___sits___ on the ___fin___ .

3.  I ___hit___ the ___bin___ .

A Look and match.

1.

2.

3.

p

h

c

op

ot

B Read and circle.

1.

mop

pop

cot

2.

dot

pot

pop

3.

top

mop

cot

4.

hop

dot

hot

C Say and choose.

1.
op

2.
ot

D Unscramble and write.

1.

c t o

_____

2.

p o t

_____

3.

o p m

_____

4.

p t o

_____

Choose and write.

op   ot

1.

h _____

2.

h _____

3.

p _____

4.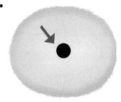

d _____

5.

m _____

6.

c _____

7.

p _____

8.

t _____

F **Read and number.**

1. The pot is hot.

2. She hops on the dot.

3. The mop is next to the cot.

G **Read and trace.**

1.  The ___pot___ is ___hot___ .

2.  She ___hops___ on the ___dot___ .

3.  The ___mop___ is next to the ___cot___ .

Unit 08 Short Vowel O

A Look and match.

1.    b   og

2.    n   od

3.    d   ox

B Read and circle.

1.
box
dog
fog

2.
fox
box
jog

3.
nod
rod
log

4.
rod
log
jog

C Say and choose.

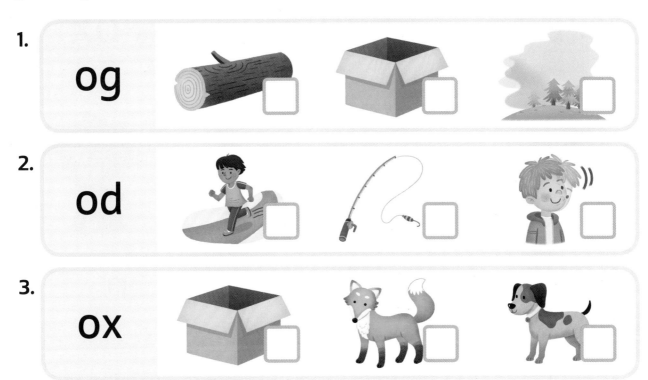

1. **og**

2. **od**

3. **ox**

D Unscramble and write.

1. o g l

2. j g o

3. o f x

4. o d n

E **Choose and write.**

og	od	ox

1.

d ____

2.

f ____

3.

n ____

4.

b ____

5.

j ____

6.

f ____

7.

l ____

8.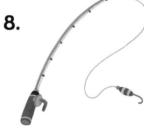

r ____

F Read and number.

1  2  3

1. The dog is in the box. ☐

2. The dog has a rod. ☐

3. The fox sits on a log. ☐

G Read and trace.

1.  The ___dog___ is in the ___box___ .

2.  The ___fox___ sits on a ___log___ .

3.  The ___dog___ has a ___rod___ .

A Look and match.

1.

   s

   un

2.

   h

   ug

3.

   m

B Read and circle.

1.

   bug
   rug
   bun

2.

   run
   fun
   rug

3.

   mug
   run
   rug

4.

   hug
   run
   sun

C Say and choose.

1.

un

2.

ug

D Unscramble and write.

1.

m g u

_____

2.

u r n

_____

3.

u n b

_____

4.

r g u

_____

E **Choose and write.**

un	ug

1.

s

2.

h

3.

r

4.

b

5.

f

6.

m

7.

b

8.

r

F **Read and number.**

1
2
3

1. The bug is on the bun.

2. The sun is fun.

3. The mug is on the rug.

G **Read and trace.**

1.  The __bug__ is on the __bun__ .

2.  The __sun__ is __fun__ .

3.  The __mug__ is on the __rug__ .

A Look and match.

1.

c · · ub

2.

h · · up

3.

s · · ut

B Read and circle.

1.

cub
sub
cup

2.

cut
tub
sub

3.

pup
cup
cut

4.

hut
nut
cub

C Say and choose.

1. ub

2. up

3. ut

D Unscramble and write.

1. u b t

2. t u n

3. u p c

4. u b c

E Choose and write.

ub	up	ut

1.

___ s ___

2.

___ c ___

3.

___ c ___

4.

___ n ___

5.

___ t ___

6.

___ p ___

7.

___ h ___

8.

___ c ___

F Read and number.

1. I cut the nut. ☐

2. The cub is in the tub. ☐

3. The pup is in the sub. ☐

G Read and trace.

1.  The ___cub___ is in the ___tub___ .

2.  I ___cut___ the ___nut___ .

3.  The ___pup___ is in the ___sub___ .

Review 2

A Look and circle.

1. **it**

2. **ug**

3. **ix**

4. **ox**
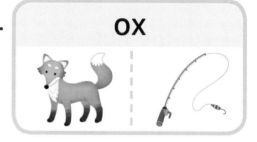

5. **up**
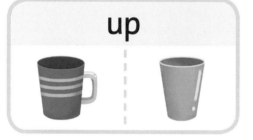

6. **od**

B Write and say.

1.
co_t_

2.
__in

3.
b__x

4.
__og

5.
b__g

6.
nu__

C Look and write.

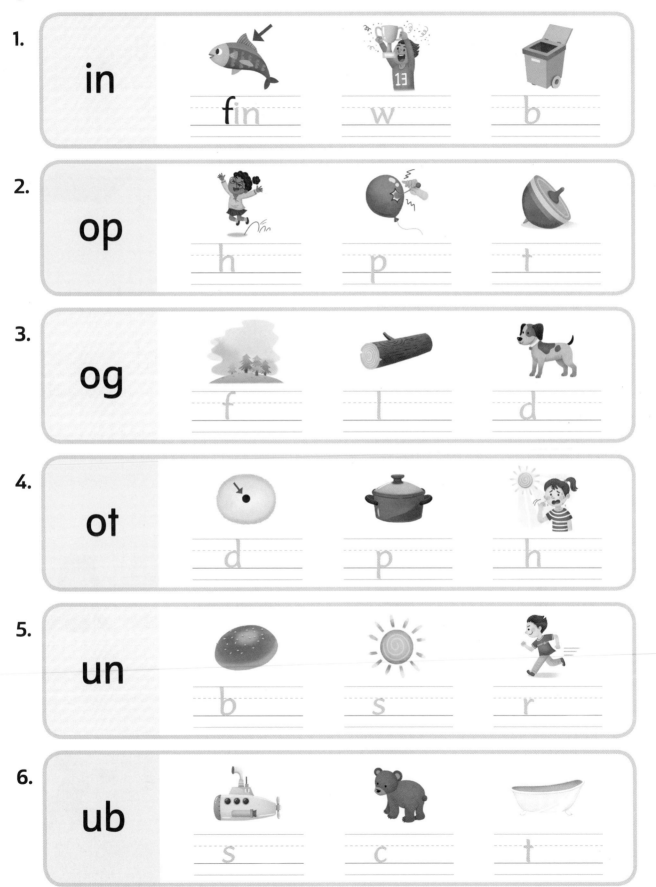

1. **in**

   f<u>in</u>   w___   b___

2. **op**

   h___   p___   t___

3. **og**

   f___   l___   d___

4. **ot**

   d___   p___   h___

5. **un**

   b___   s___   r___

6. **ub**

   s___   c___   t___

Final Review

● **Choose and write.**

an at am ap en et ed eg

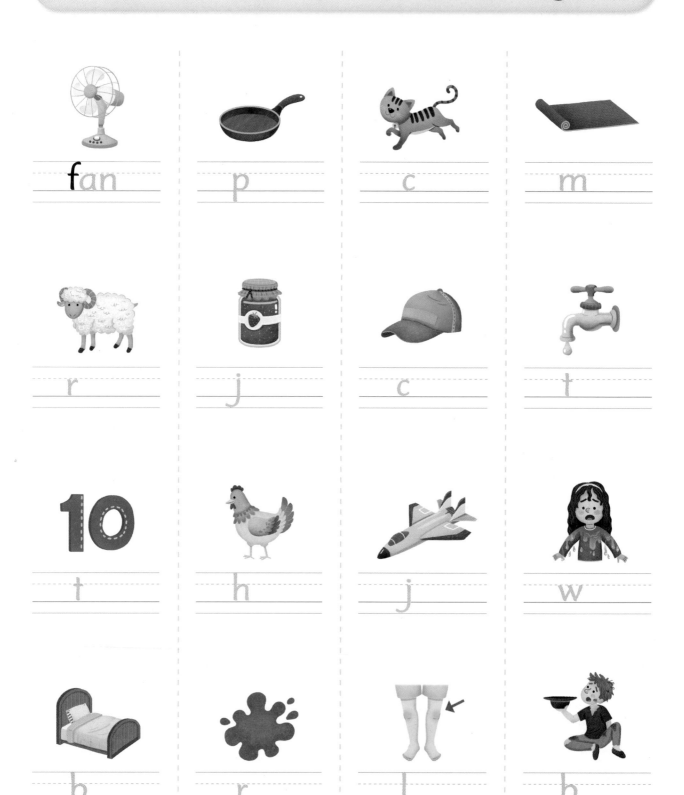

fan	p____	c____	m____
r____	j____	c____	t____
t____	h____	j____	w____
b____	r____	l____	b____

ig id ip in it ix op ot

b_____

p_____

k_____

l_____

d_____

l_____

f_____

p_____

s_____

h_____

f_____

s_____

t_____

m_____

p_____

h_____

Final Review

og   od   ox   un   ug   ub   up   ut

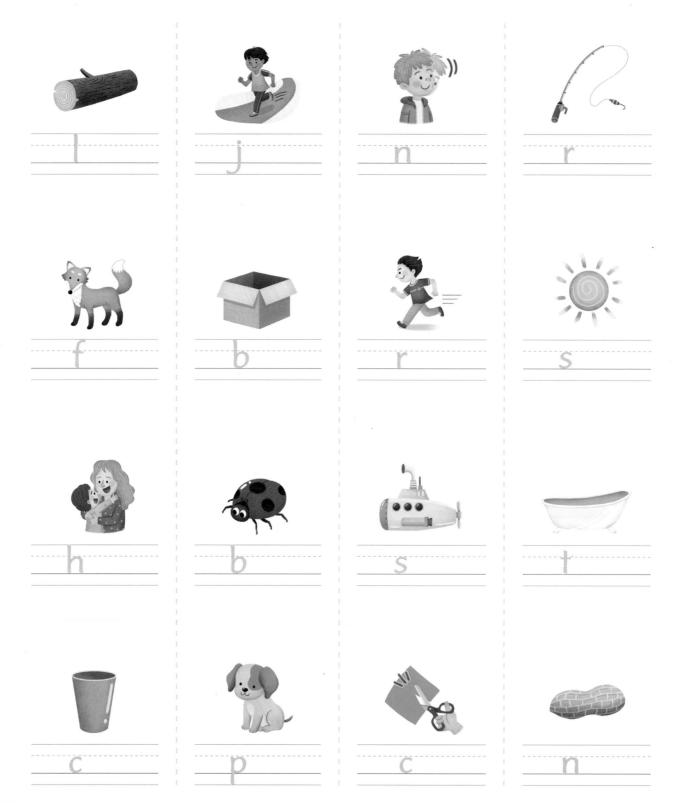

l___ j___ n___ r___

f___ b___ r___ s___

h___ b___ s___ t___

c___ p___ c___ n___